A FOCUS ON...

FEELINGS

By John Wood

©2018
Book Life
King's Lynn
Norfolk PE30 4LS

ISBN: 978-1-78637-252-9

All rights reserved
Printed in Malaysia

Written by:
John Wood

Edited by:
Kirsty Holmes

Designed by:
Danielle Rippengill

A catalogue record for this book is available from the British Library

PHOTO CREDITS

Abbreviations: l–left, r–right, b–bottom, t–top, c–centre, m–middle.

2 – Yuganov Konstantin. 6 – Gelpi. 9 – Gelpi. 11 – Oksana Kuzmina. 13 – Photobac. 15 – Martin Novak. 17 – TADAphotographer. 19 – Morrowind. 21 – Trifonenkolvan. 22 – wavebreakmedia.

Images are courtesy of Shutterstock.com.
With thanks to Getty Images, Thinkstock Photo and iStockphoto.

CONTENTS

Page 4	Writing Down Our Feelings
Page 6	What Are Feelings?
Page 8	Excited
Page 10	Proud
Page 12	Jealous
Page 14	Angry
Page 16	Sad
Page 18	Scared
Page 20	Calm
Page 22	Happy
Page 24	Glossary and Index

Words that look like this can be found in the glossary on page 24.

Writing Down Our Feelings

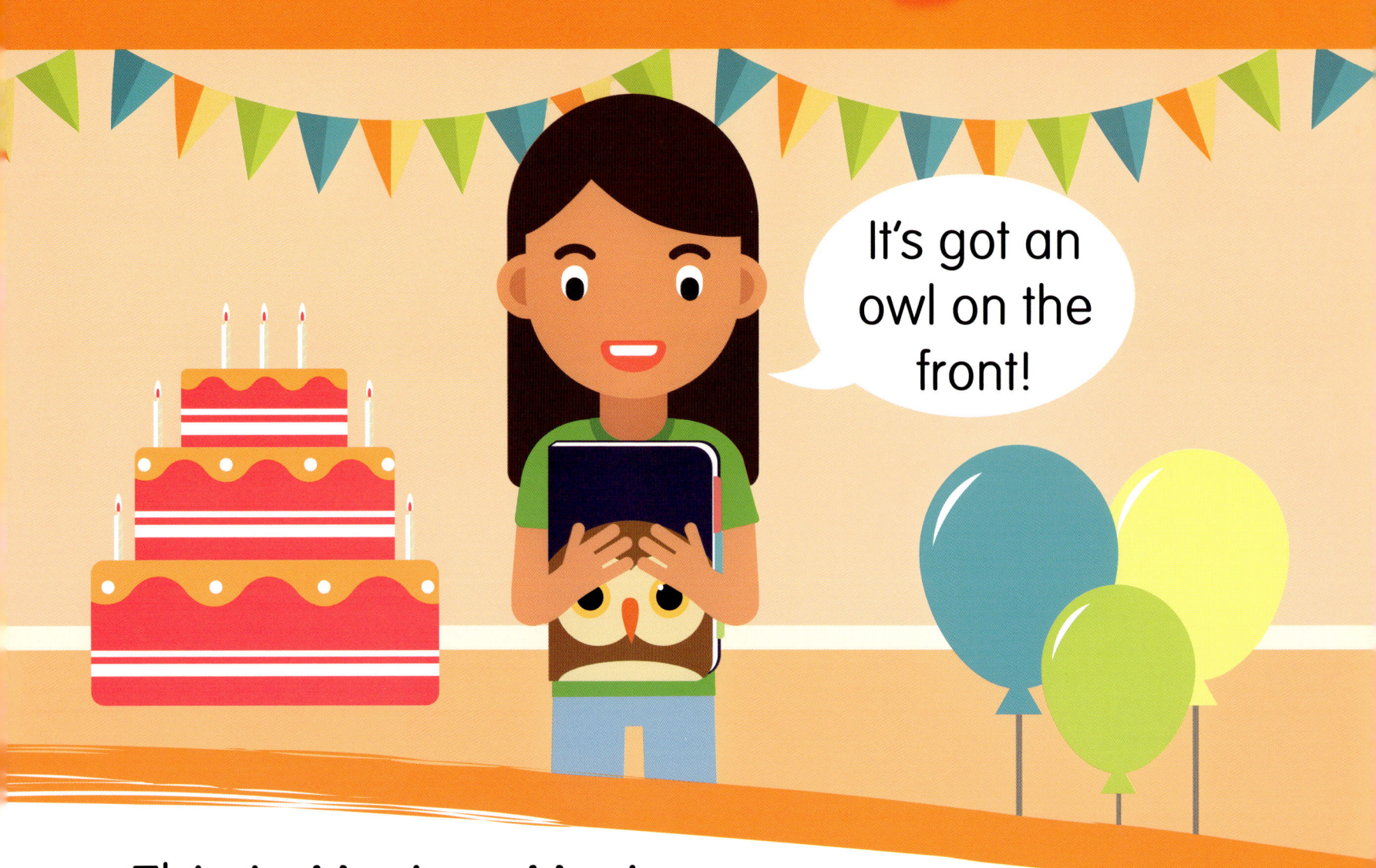

"It's got an owl on the front!"

This is Marina. Marina was given a **diary** for her birthday.

Marina likes to write down all her feelings in the diary.

She has lots of different feelings every day.

What Are Feelings?

Feelings can change the way we **behave**.

Feelings come from our thoughts, but they can make our bodies feel different too.

Marina would like to show us her diary.

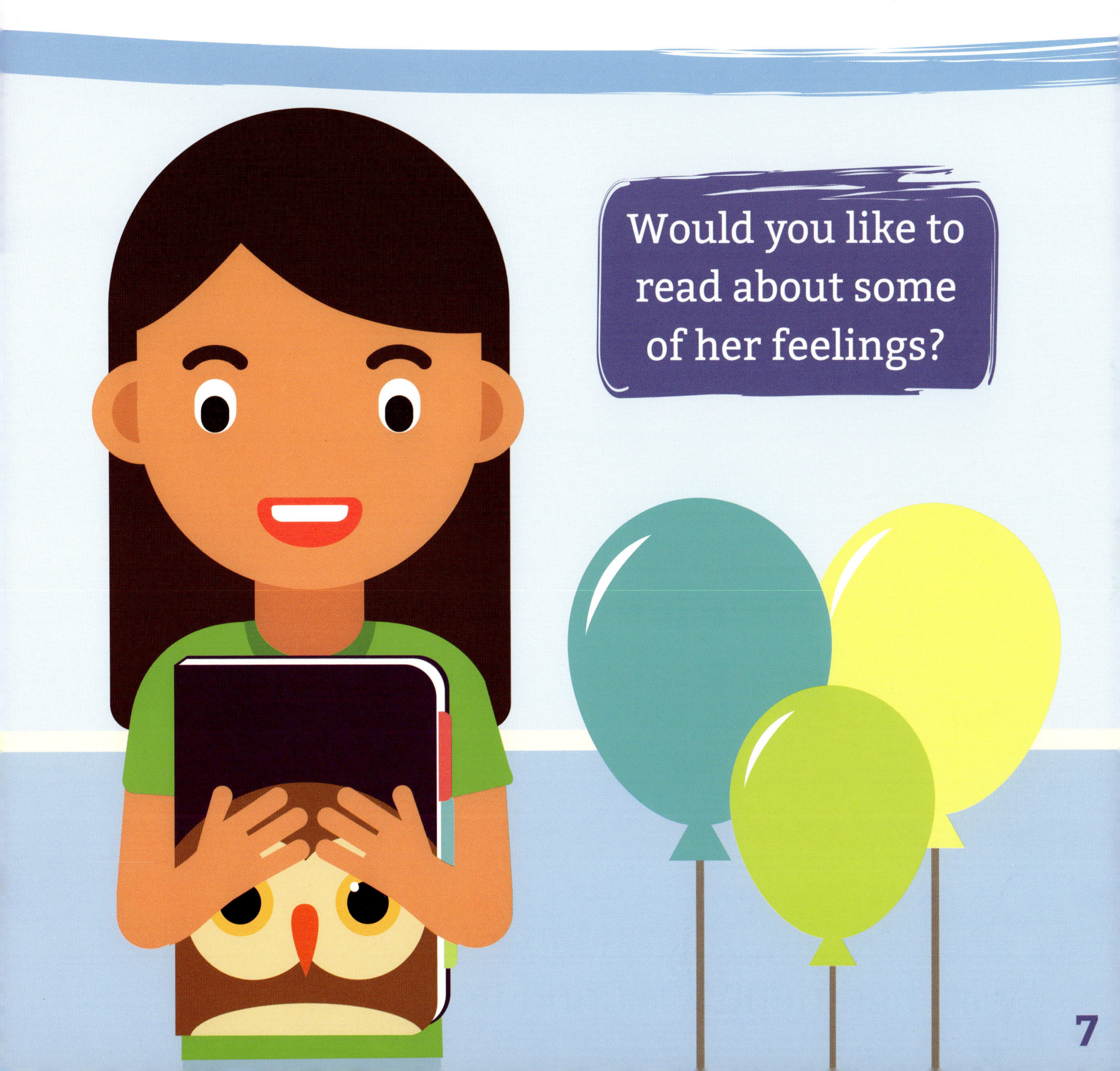

Would you like to read about some of her feelings?

Excited

On Monday, Marina played pass-the-parcel with her friends. Marina felt excited.

When you are excited, your heart might beat faster. You might want to laugh and jump around.

Being excited is fun!

Proud

I used all the colours.

On Tuesday, Marina painted a picture. Marina felt proud.

You might be proud when you do something good. You might have a **rising** feeling in your chest.

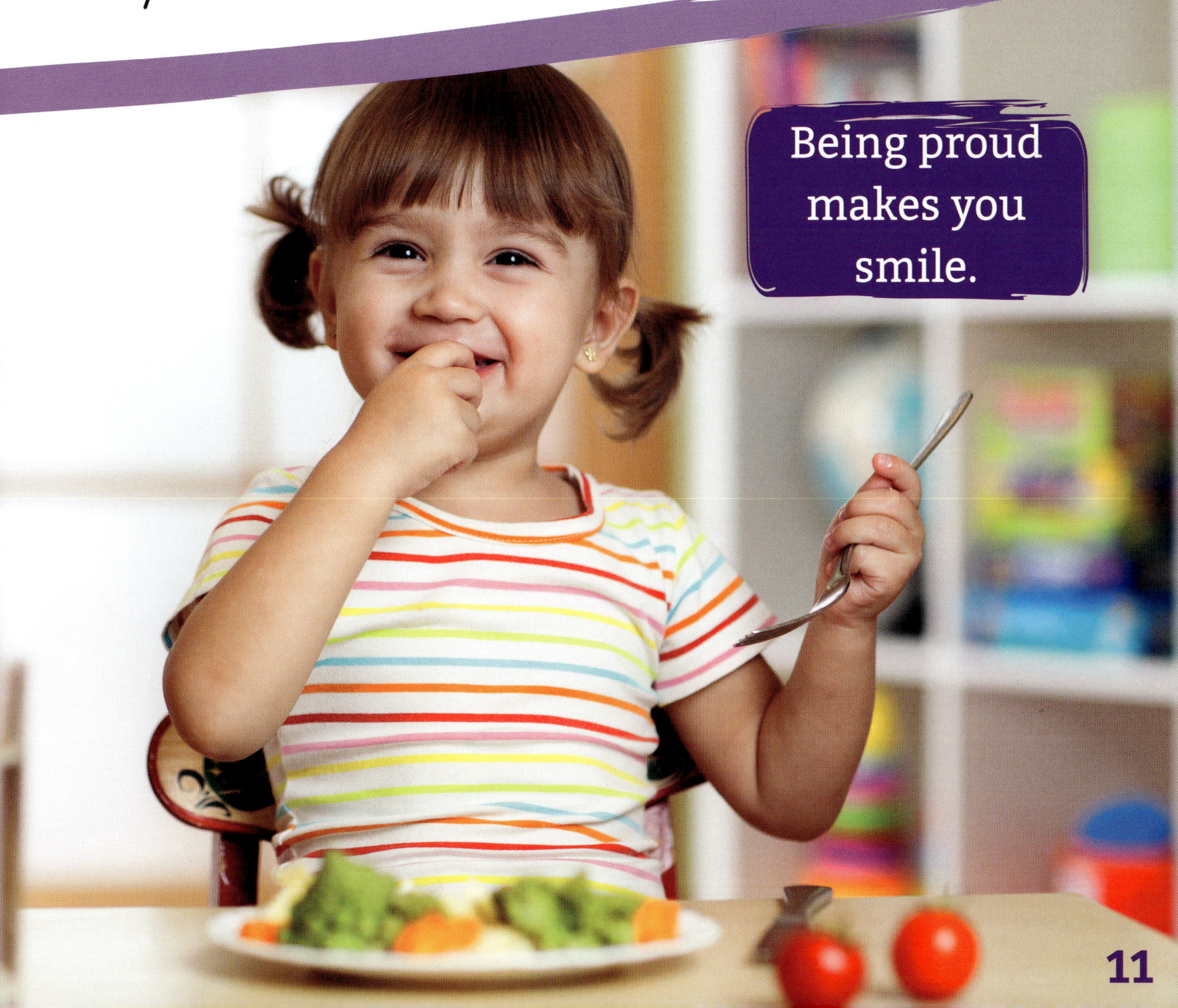

Being proud makes you smile.

Jealous

Being jealous doesn't feel nice at all.

Marina felt jealous of Charlotte. Marina wished she could paint as well as Charlotte.

Sometimes we feel jealous when we want what other people have.

Try to think about what you do have, instead of what you don't.

Angry

"I want ice-cream!"

On Wednesday, Marina wasn't allowed any ice-cream. She had to eat a banana instead. Marina felt angry.

When you are angry, your skin might feel hot. You might want to hit things and shout.

It is important to never hit or shout at other people.

Sad

Marina has lost her favourite teddy bear!

Marina looked everywhere, but she couldn't find her bear. Marina felt sad.

When you feel sad, you might want to cry. You might have a heavy feeling in your chest.

It might help to draw a picture of what is making you feel sad.

Scared

Marina feels scared!

Thursday night, Marina thought she heard a monster. It sounded a lot like an owl.

When you feel scared, your stomach might feel busy and sick. You might want to hide or run away.

Telling someone why you are scared will help.

Calm

The park was warm and quiet.

On Friday, Marina went to the park after school. She felt calm.

When you feel calm, you don't have any strong feelings. You might want to be quiet and **peaceful**.

Being calm is a nice feeling.

Happy

What feelings do you have? You could write about them in a diary.

We feel happy when we do things we like. It makes us want to laugh and smile.

Marina liked showing us her diary.
She feels happy.

Now she can write about today in her diary too!

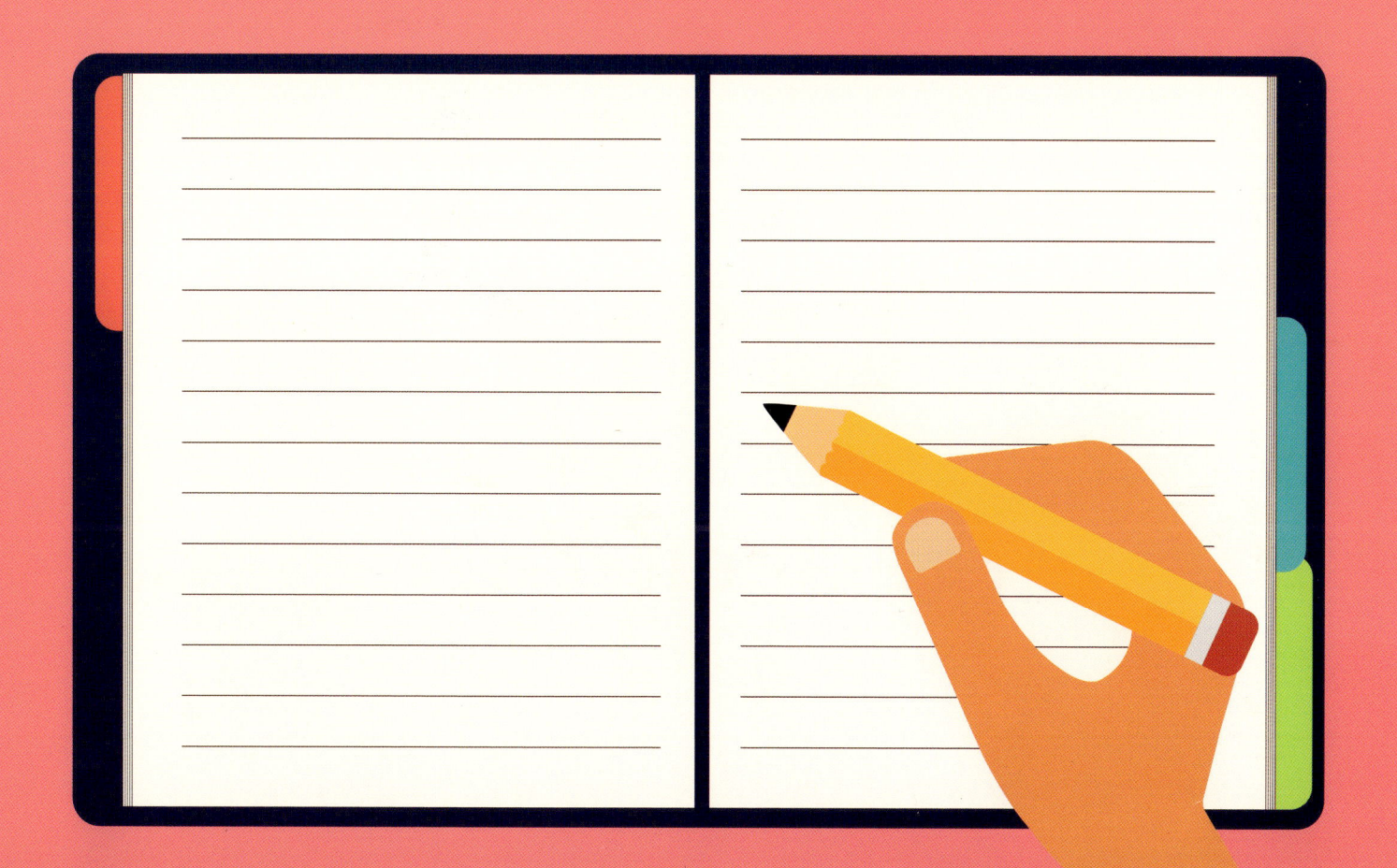

Glossary:

behave act in a certain way

diary a book for writing about things in your life

peaceful nice and quiet

rising going up

Index:

chest 11, 17

laugh 9, 22

quiet 20–21

shout 15

smile 11, 22

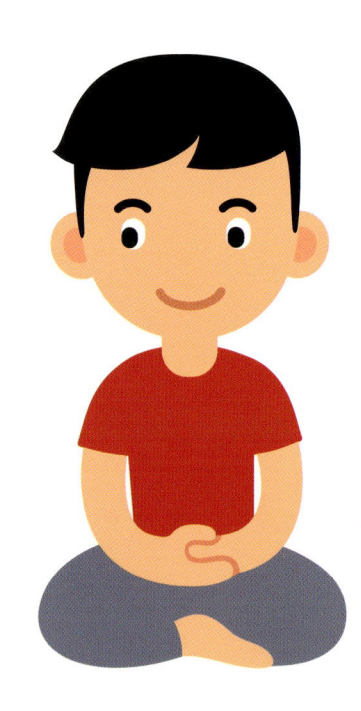